POINTS OF VIEW

Should Animal TESTING Be Banned?

By Riley Lawrence

KidHaven
PUBLISHING

Published in 2019 by
KidHaven Publishing, an Imprint of Greenhaven Publishing, LLC
353 3rd Avenue
Suite 255
New York, NY 10010

Designer: Deanna Paternostro
Editor: Katie Kawa

Photo credits: Cover Kirill Kurashov/Shutterstock.com; p. 4 PETA/Wikimedia Commons; pp. 5 (top), 13 Gorodenkoff/Shutterstock.com; p. 5 (bottom) ADRIAN DENNIS/AFP/Getty Images; p. 6 Vorobyeva/Shutterstock.com; p. 7 PA Images via Getty Images; pp. 9, 21 (inset, left) Jose Gil/Shutterstock.com; p. 11 unoL/Shutterstock.com; p. 15 Zoriana Zaitseva/Shutterstock.com; p. 17 niderlander/Shutterstock.com; p. 19 Aomboon/Shutterstock.com; p. 21 (notepad) ESB Professional/Shutterstock.com; p. 21 (markers) Kucher Serhii/Shutterstock.com; p. 21 (photo frame) FARBAI/iStock/Thinkstock; p. 21 (inset, middle-left) anyaivanova/Shutterstock.com; p. 21 (inset, middle-right) Alberto Pezzali/NurPhoto via Getty Images; p. 21 (inset, right) Anil Kumar Shakya/Pacific Press/LightRocket via Getty Images.

Library of Congress Cataloging-in-Publication Data

Names: Lawrence, Riley, 1993- author.
Title: Should animal testing be banned? / Riley Lawrence.
Description: New York : KidHaven Publishing, [2019] | Series: Points of view | Includes bibliographical references and index.
Identifiers: LCCN 2018027560 (print) | LCCN 2018029596 (ebook) | ISBN 9781534527928 (eBook) | ISBN 9781534527911 (library bound book : alk. paper) | ISBN 9781534527898 (pbk. book : alk. paper) | ISBN 9781534527904 (6 pack : alk. paper)
Subjects: LCSH: Animal experimentation–Juvenile literature. | Laboratory animals–Juvenile literature. | Animal welfare–Juvenile literature.
Classification: LCC HV4915 (ebook) | LCC HV4915 .L39 2019 (print) | DDC 179/.4–dc23
LC record available at https://lccn.loc.gov/2018027560

Printed in the United States of America

CPSIA compliance information: Batch #BW19KL: For further information contact Greenhaven Publishing LLC, New York, New York at 1-844-317-7404.

Please visit our website, www.greenhavenpublishing.com. For a free color catalog of all our high-quality books, call toll free 1-844-317-7404 or fax 1-844-317-7405.

CONTENTS

An Important ISSUE

Animals are often used to help people. They give people food, they carry people and goods, and they even help people make scientific discoveries. Scientists often use animals in different kinds of tests. Many of these tests help people learn if drugs and other products are safe to use.

Some people feel animal testing should be banned. They believe animals have rights and shouldn't be put in danger to help people. Others believe animal testing is important and has saved many human lives. Read on to learn more about this **debate**!

Know the Facts!

One group that often speaks out against animal testing and in favor of animal rights is People for the Ethical Treatment of Animals (PETA).

It's important to understand the facts used by both sides of the animal testing debate. That's the only way to have an informed, or educated, opinion about this issue.

In the LAB

Animal testing often happens in a laboratory, which is a place where scientists **perform** experiments. In many of these tests, animals are given drugs or other **medical treatments** to see what they do to a living thing. In some cases, scientists also give the animals different sicknesses to see if a drug will make that sickness go away.

These tests can lead to the creation of new, lifesaving drugs. Many of the most important medical advances in history started with tests on animals. However, animal testing can also hurt or even kill the animals used in the tests.

Know the Facts!

Many beauty products, such as soaps and makeup, are also tested on animals.

Scientists have been performing laboratory tests—often shortened to lab tests—on animals for hundreds of years.

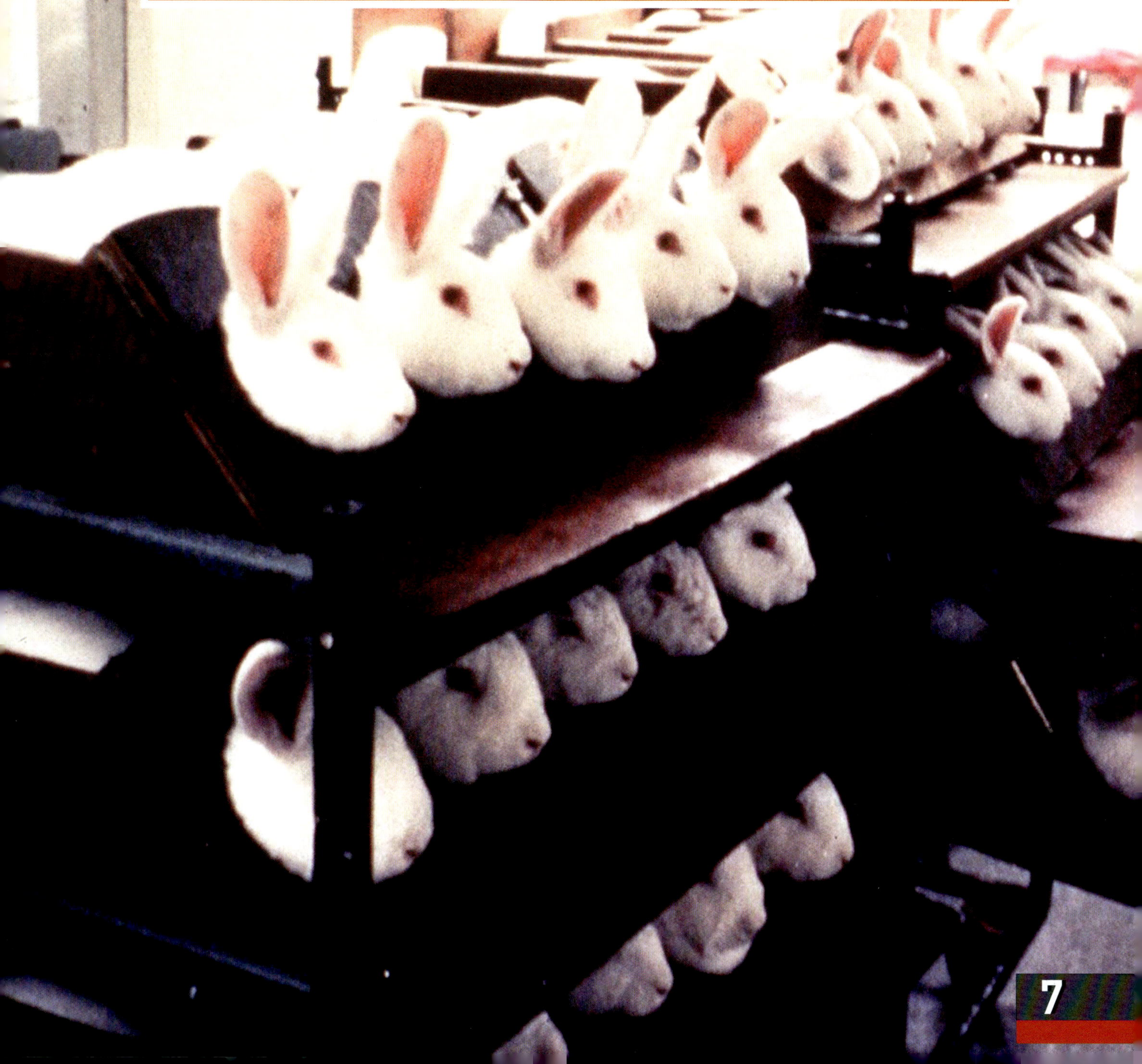

Saving Human LIVES

Scientists use animal testing because they believe it's the only way to know how a drug or other product **affects** a living thing without harming people. The animals chosen for testing often have body systems that are like those found in a human. This way, scientists can see how those systems are affected without having to **risk** human lives.

Scientists often argue that animal testing is the best and safest way to create new medical treatments. Throughout history, animal testing has saved millions of human lives, which scientists believe is the **goal** of this kind of **research**.

Know the Facts!

Scientists often study pig hearts when they want to know more about human hearts. This is because a pig's heart is a lot like a human's heart.

Animal testing saves human lives. Many people believe this is the main reason why it shouldn't be banned.

Harming Animals to HELP HUMANS

People who support animal testing generally believe that the good things it can lead to are worth the possible harm that can come to animals. Other people strongly disagree. These people believe animals' lives have just as much value as humans' lives. They think it's wrong to put animals in danger to help people.

Animal testing can make animals sick or cause them pain, which many people believe is wrong. Supporters of the animal rights movement also want to ban animal testing because they believe animals should live freely in nature and not in laboratories.

Know the Facts!

A 2015 study showed that as many as 100 million animals are used in laboratory tests every year.

People who fight to ban animal testing believe these experiments cause animals to suffer and often die to help humans, which they feel isn't fair to animals.

The Only WAY

Scientists know that harm sometimes comes to animals during scientific tests, but they believe there's no other way to do their important work. Many tests require a living body to make sure a drug or other product works correctly or is safe for people to use.

Some people believe computer models could be used for tests instead of animals. Supporters of animal testing have argued that these models aren't always accurate, or correct. In fact, scientists often use computers and live experiments together to get the best results, which means animal testing still needs to take place.

Know the Facts!

The U.S. Food and Drug Administration (FDA) is the part of the government in charge of making sure drugs are safe for people to use.

Some scientists believe computer models aren't advanced enough to replace live animals in scientific experiments.

New Testing METHODS

Computer models aren't always accurate, but neither is animal testing. People who want to ban animal testing often point to the fact that these experiments don't always accurately show how a drug will affect people. In fact, more than 90 percent of drugs that pass the animal testing part of research fail when tested on humans.

Other kinds of tests could also be used instead of computer models or animal testing. New ways to study human cells have made it easier to safely test how drugs affect those cells without needing to use animals.

Know the Facts!

A new testing method called microdosing happens when people are given a very small amount of a drug—too small to cause any harm—and are studied to see how it affects their body.

Many scientists are working hard to come up with ways to replace animal testing.

A Look at the LAW

Although many people have spoken out against animal testing, it's not illegal. In fact, laws exist to make sure many animals used for scientific research are treated with respect and care.

For example, the Animal Welfare Act (AWA) became a law in 1966. The AWA set rules for how animals used for research should be treated. It's the only federal, or national, law in the United States governing animal testing. However, many states have passed laws to limit animal testing, especially for beauty products. **Inspectors** often check laboratories to make sure these laws are being followed.

Know the Facts!

More than 30 countries around the world have passed laws to ban or limit animal testing for beauty products.

The AWA was created to make sure certain animals used in experiments are given proper food, water, and medical care when it's needed.

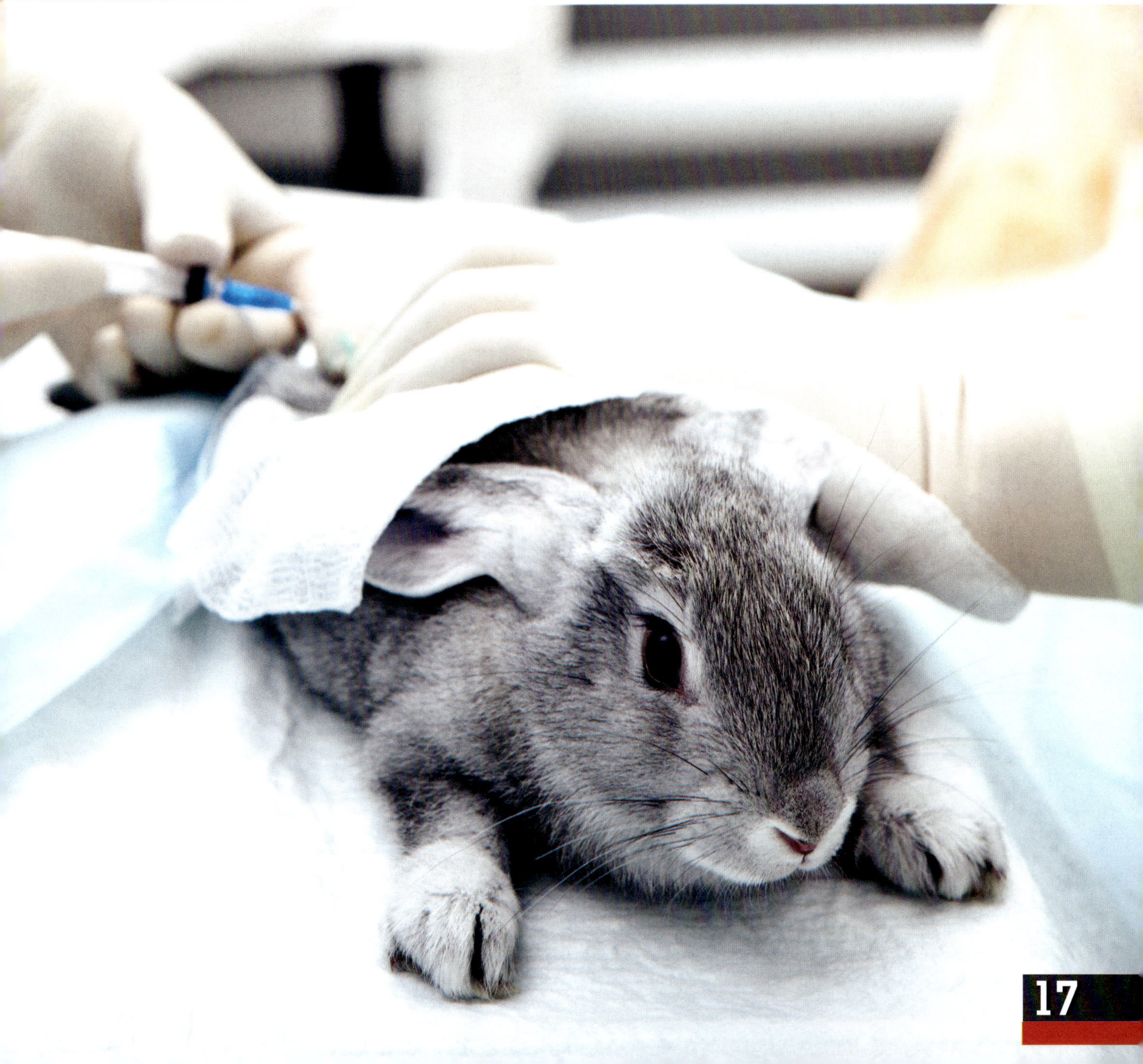

Not Everything Is PROTECTED

Although laws exist to make animal testing as safe as possible, these laws don't apply to all animals. For example, the AWA doesn't **protect** rats or mice. Studies have shown that up to 95 percent of all animal testing is done using rats and mice. This means that 95 percent of laboratory animals aren't protected by the AWA.

People who speak out against animal testing believe it's not fair for some animals to be protected by laws while others aren't. They feel the only way to be sure all animals are treated well is to ban animal testing completely.

Know the Facts!

A 2015 study showed that 50 percent of Americans dislike animal testing, while 47 percent of Americans support it.

Rats and mice can feel pain just like other animals can. This is why many people believe they should be protected by the AWA or not used in experiments at all.

Your Place in

THE DEBATE

Animal testing is an important issue to talk about because it affects so many areas of our lives. Banning animal testing would change the way scientists study many things, including drugs and other medical treatments. It would also change how some beauty products are made. Some companies have already stopped testing their beauty products on animals.

People often feel very strongly about animal rights issues such as animal testing. After learning the facts about animal testing, how do you feel? Should this kind of testing be banned?

Know the Facts!

Some beauty products have a label that says they're not tested on animals or are **cruelty-free**. Although people often believe these labels, they're not clearly defined. This means the products might still have things in them that were once tested on animals.

Should animal testing be banned?

YES	NO
• Animal testing can kill animals, and they shouldn't be put in danger to help humans.	• Animal testing saves human lives.
• Other kinds of testing exist that don't harm animals.	• Computer models and other tests aren't as accurate as animal testing.
• Laws don't protect all animals used in experiments.	• Laws exist to make sure animal testing is as safe as possible.
• Animal testing often isn't accurate because laboratory animals aren't the same as people.	• Banning animal testing would be hard because it would completely change the way scientists work.

A chart such as this one can help you understand different points of view and form your own.

GLOSSARY

affect: To produce an effect on something.

cruelty-free: Created without harmful testing on animals.

debate: An argument or discussion about an issue, generally between two sides.

goal: Purpose.

inspector: Someone who looks at something carefully in order to learn more about it or find problems with it.

medical treatment: Care given to a person or animal that is sick.

perform: To do something that requires a skill.

protect: To keep safe.

research: Careful study that is done to find and report new knowledge about something.

risk: To put in danger.

For More INFORMATION

WEBSITES

CBBC Newsround Science Debates: Animal Testing
news.bbc.co.uk/cbbcnews/hi/find_out/guides/tech/science_debates/newsid_2173000/2173934.stm
This website helps explain how people in Great Britain view the animal testing debate and other issues by breaking down both sides and providing links to other popular science debates.

PETA Kids
www.petakids.com
Kids who are interested in learning more about animal testing and other animal rights issues can visit PETA's website.

BOOKS

Alkire, Jessie. *Animal Experimentation*. Minneapolis, MN: Checkerboard Library, 2018.

Parker, Vic. *Let's Think About Animal Rights*. Chicago, IL: Capstone Heinemann Library, 2015.

Terp, Gail. *The Debate About Animal Testing*. Lake Elmo, MN: Focus Readers, 2018.

INDEX